DKfindout!

Climate
Change

Author: Maryam Sharif-Draper
Consultant: Dr. Stephen Burnley

Senior editors Carrie Love, Roohi Sehgal
Project editor Kritika Gupta
Assistant editors Becky Walsh, Niharika Prabhakar
US Senior editor Shannon Beatty
Project art editors Charlotte Bull, Roohi Rais
Art editor Mohd Zishan
Assistant art editor Bhagyashree Nayak
DTP designers Sachin Gupta, Vijay Kandwal
Project picture researcher Sakshi Saluja
Jacket co-ordinator Issy Walsh
Jacket designer Rashika Kachroo
Managing editors Penny Smith, Monica Saigal
Managing art editor Mabel Chan
Deputy Managing art editor Ivy Sengupta
Producer, pre-production Heather Blagden
Senior producer Ena Matagic
Delhi team head Malavika Talukder
Publishing manager Francesca Young
Creative directors Helen Senior, Clare Baggaley
Publishing director Sarah Larter

Educational consultant Jacqueline Harris

First American Edition, 2020
Published in the United States by DK Publishing
1450 Broadway, Suite 801, New York, NY 10018

A catalog record for this book
is available from the Library of Congress.
ISBN: 978-1-4654-9314-9 (Paperback)
ISBN: 978-1-4654-9315-6 (Hardcover)

DK books are available at special discounts when purchased
in bulk for sales promotions, premiums, fund-raising, or educational
use. For details, contact: DK Publishing Special Markets,
1450 Broadway, Suite 801, New York, NY 10018
SpecialSales@dk.com

Printed and bound in China

A WORLD OF IDEAS:
SEE ALL THERE IS TO KNOW

www.dk.com

Contents

Sustainable
utensils

Cloth bag for groceries

Green sea
turtle

Growing radishes

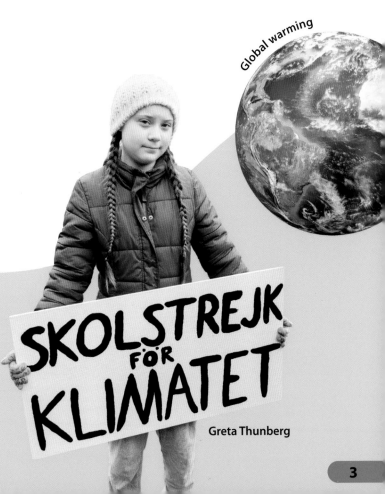
Global warming

Walruses

SKOLSTREJK FÖR KLIMATET

Greta Thunberg

What is climate?

Climate is the average weather conditions in one place over a long period of time. This includes the amount of rainfall, hours of sunshine, and temperature. The Earth's climate has varied naturally in the past, but now it is changing more rapidly than ever.

Climate change
The Earth is heating up, which means this polar ice is melting.

What affects climate?

Different parts of the Earth experience their own very different climates. These are affected by a variety of factors:

Mountains are often snow covered.

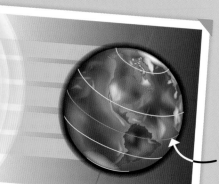

Distance from the equator
Areas of land that are farther away from the equator are much colder. The Earth's curves mean that the sun's rays are spread out over a much larger area of land closer to the poles.

Equator
An imaginary line that runs horizontally around the middle of the Earth.

Height above sea level
The higher land is above the oceans, the lower its temperature. At the top of Mount Everest, the temperature never goes above freezing!

Summer homes are often by the sea.

Wind can pick up clouds from the ocean and bring them inland.

Distance from the sea
Oceans heat up and cool down much more slowly than land. As a result, places near the coast tend to be cooler in the summer and warmer in the winter.

Wind direction
Wind blowing from the ocean can bring frequent rainfall, whereas inland wind can create desert microclimates.

Climate through time

The Earth's climate has continually changed through time. Natural events—such as variations in the Earth's orbit of the sun, volcanic eruptions, and the impact of meteorites—have caused these changes. To predict change in the future, we can look at what has happened to our climate in the past.

Human impact on climate

Unlike climate change in the past, the current rise in global temperature is mostly the result of human activity. Burning fossil fuels and deforestation are causing a dramatic increase in greenhouse gas emissions (see pages 8–9).

Break up of Pangea

300 million years ago, Earth's continents were joined together as a supercontinent, called Pangea. As Earth's tectonic plates began to move, Pangea began to break apart. Plate tectonic movement also caused volcanic eruptions and earthquakes.

Dinosaurs on Earth

As Pangea began to separate, the Earth's climate changed with it. Temperatures dropped and rainfall increased. As more plants grew, dinosaurs began to roam the land. Snakes, insects, and flowering plants also began to appear.

Ice ages

During an ice age, thick sheets of ice cover large areas of land. The Earth has had a number of ice ages in the past, sometimes lasting millions of years. Ice changed the surface of the Earth, eroding land and causing many of the Earth's lakes to form.

Volcanic eruptions

In the past, explosive volcanic eruptions have changed the Earth's climate. As smoke and ash were spewed from craters around the world, changes in the atmosphere caused temperatures to alter.

Around 252 million years ago, Pangea suffered a mass extinction known as the Great Dying. Most species that lived on the supercontinent became extinct.

As land continued separating, dinosaurs continued to evolve. But the changing climate caused many to die. Then 66 million years ago, an asteroid collided with Earth, causing the extinction of all the dinosaurs.

Animals that lived during an ice age were adapted to the extremely cold, dry conditions. Woolly mammoths had long hair to keep warm and huge tusks to help them look for food under the snow.

Scientists think that large volcanic eruptions may have been the cause of mass extinctions in the past. Because conditions changed quickly, living things did not have time to adapt, so they died.

The greenhouse effect

The gases in our atmosphere trap the sun's heat, just like the roof of a greenhouse. Without this natural greenhouse effect, the Earth's surface would be covered in ice—much too cold for life to exist.

Heat energy from the sun's rays

Energy reflected back by the Earth's atmosphere

Energy reflected back by the clouds

Earth's atmosphere

Heat from the sun
The Earth's climate system is controlled by heat energy, which reaches the Earth through the sun's rays.

Absorbing energy
About 70 percent of the sun's energy passes through our atmosphere. Some of it is absorbed by the oceans and land.

Energy absorbed by oceans and land

Energy reflected back by the Earth

Enhanced greenhouse effect

Human activity, such as burning fossil fuels and deforestation, is releasing more and more greenhouse gases. As a result, the amount of heat becoming trapped by the atmosphere is increasing.

What is global warming?

Earth's climate is changing. As humans continue to release greenhouse gases into the atmosphere, the average temperature of the Earth is increasing. This global warming is causing extreme weather, changes to natural habitats, a rise in sea levels, and a range of other effects.

Widespread deforestation causes a rise in greenhouse gases.

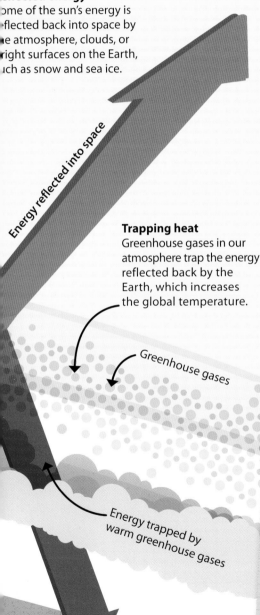

Reflected energy
Some of the sun's energy is reflected back into space by the atmosphere, clouds, or bright surfaces on the Earth, such as snow and sea ice.

Energy reflected into space

Trapping heat
Greenhouse gases in our atmosphere trap the energy reflected back by the Earth, which increases the global temperature.

Greenhouse gases

Energy trapped by warm greenhouse gases

Greenhouse gases

Some of the gases in our atmosphere trap energy from the sun's rays. The main ones are carbon dioxide, methane, nitrous oxide, and water vapor.

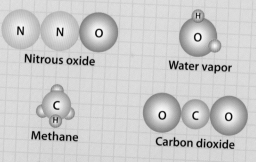

Nitrous oxide

Water vapor

Methane

Carbon dioxide

Carbon dioxide is the most common—and dangerous—greenhouse gas.

Fossil fuels

Buried beneath layer upon layer of rock and other minerals in the ground is a reserve of coal, oil, and natural gas. Formed over hundreds of millions of years, from dead plants and animals, these materials are known as fossil fuels. Today, much of the world's energy comes from these fuels. However, the excess burning of these fossil fuels harms the environment and our health.

Pollution

When burned in huge quantities, fossil fuels release polluting greenhouse gases into our atmosphere. Fossil fuels are the largest source of carbon dioxide, the most common greenhouse gas.

CO_2

Oil rigs

As the demand for oil increases, companies are looking under the ocean floor for oil reserves. Rigs, such as this one, are gigantic machines that drill down underground and extract oil. When accidents happen on rigs, they can lead to pollution of the oceans and coastlines.

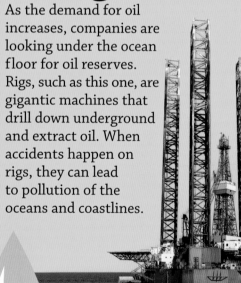

TRANSPORTATION

Fossil fuels may have to travel long distances from where they are extracted to where they are used. Transporting flammable fuel risks accidents and produces even more pollution.

Large tanke carrying fue

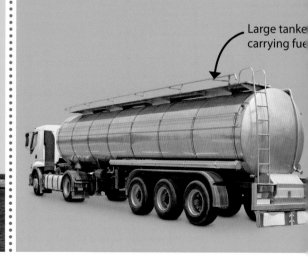

MINING FOR FOSSIL FUELS

To extract buried coal, miners dig deep underground. Yet this is dangerous, both for people and the environment, with risks of landslides, flooding, and water contamination.

Fracking

A process called fracking is used to extract hard-to-reach fossil fuels. A powerful jet of water breaks apart underground rock, which releases the fuels. This can cause a number of problems, such as frequent earthquakes and water contamination.

Nonrenewable future

We now know that at the rate we are currently using fossil fuels, it is only a matter of time before they completely run out. Fossil fuels form over a long period of time, so it is impossible for us to replace them soon.

Industrial Revolution

The 18th and 19th centuries were an exciting time of great inventions. However, to power factories, coal, and later on other fossil fuels such as oil and gas, were burned. Since the Industrial Revolution, the amount of greenhouse gases in the atmosphere has risen to dangerous levels.

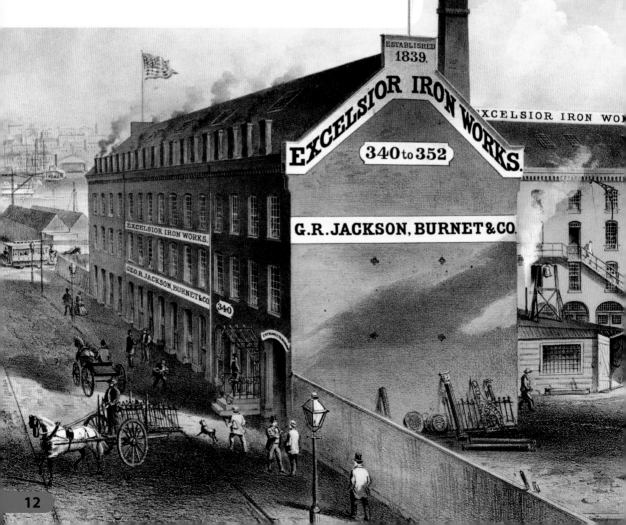

Smoke in the sky
The burning of fossil fuels
released large amounts of
pollution into the atmosphere
including smoke and carbon
dioxide (CO_2).

Changes during the Industrial Revolution

New inventions changed people's lives around the world. The battery, the sewing machine, and the telephone were all invented at this time.

Working in a factory

Factories
Huge factories were built to produce goods such as clothing, shoes, pottery, and glassware. The new machinery was much quicker than human labor, meaning products were less expensive and so more people could buy them.

Steam engine locomotive

Transportation
In a steam engine, water is heated in a large tank to make steam. The steam helps make the engine move. Steam engines were used in factories, mines, trains, and steamboats.

The ozone layer

The atmosphere that surrounds the Earth is made up of several layers. Part of the layer known as the stratosphere contains ozone gas. Although this ozone layer is thin, it acts as a protective shield by absorbing almost all of the harmful ultraviolet radiation that is traveling to the Earth from the sun.

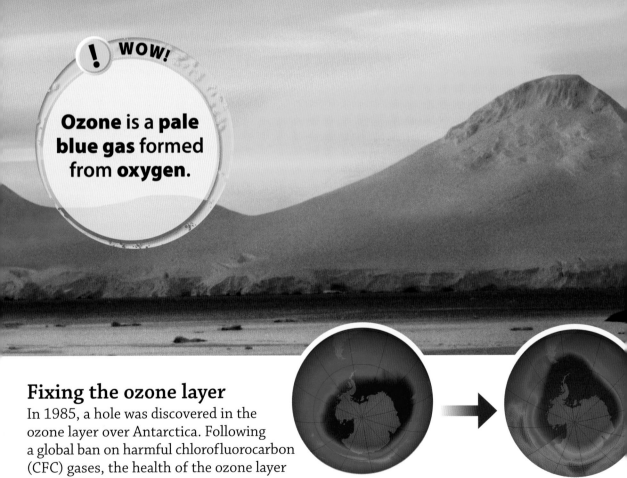

! WOW!

Ozone is a **pale blue gas** formed from **oxygen.**

Fixing the ozone layer

In 1985, a hole was discovered in the ozone layer over Antarctica. Following a global ban on harmful chlorofluorocarbon (CFC) gases, the health of the ozone layer is improving quickly.

2010

2012

Protecting the Earth
The ozone stops all living things on the Earth from being burned by the sun.

The hole in the ozone layer
Scientists discovered that CFC gases, which were found in aerosol sprays and refrigerators, were causing the hole in the ozone layer to open.

Montreal Protocol
In 1987, countries around the world met in Montreal in Canada and agreed to protect the ozone layer. They banned the use and production of CFCs, which would allow the ozone to recover.

Aerosol spray cans

Launching a weather balloon

The road to recovery
Thanks to the Montreal Protocol, the ozone layer is on the mend. Weather balloons were launched to keep track of the ozone, but satellites are more often used now. Scientists think that the hole will disappear by 2060.

2015

2017

2019

Transportation

Traveling from A to B in vehicles is one of the biggest causes of climate change. Most of our transportation relies on fossil fuels, which release carbon dioxide (CO_2) and other pollutants into the atmosphere. As a result, people around the world are being encouraged to walk or bicycle.

Flying around

Over 100,000 flights leave airports around the world every day! Airplane travel is a huge contributor to climate change.

Diesel trains
Harmful gases are released.

Trains powered by fossil fuels are being replaced by electric trains.

On the road

Most gas and diesel cars are powered by fossil fuels, which release harmful carbon dioxide into the atmosphere. Electric cars are more environmentally friendly, because they release no pollution.

Train travel

Railroads need a lot of energy. Although fewer trains use fossil fuels in their engines now, train travel relies on electricity, which sometimes involves burning fossil fuels.

Traffic jams release high amounts of pollution.

Huge cargo ships take fruit, vegetables, and other foods all around the world.

Food miles

By looking at the distance food travels from where it is made to where it is eaten, we can look at the impact our food has on the environment.

Taking the bus

Buses are a big contributor to air pollution, but a bus full of passengers is about 10 times less polluting than if they all traveled by car.

Clean transportation

Electric-powered vehicles and biofuels are growing in popularity. Made from renewable and sustainable natural materials, biofuels are much better for the environment.

Growing algae fuel

How much travel produces $2^1/_5$ lb (1 kg) of CO_2?

The amount of carbon dioxide released into the atmosphere depends on the mode of transportation that is used. Look at these types of transportation. Which ones do you use? How can you contribute less to CO_2 emissions?

2 miles (4 km)

9 miles (14 km)

15 miles (24 km)

11 miles (18 km)

9 miles (14 km)

43 miles (70 km)

What we buy

From expensive gadgets and fashionable clothes to disposable food packaging and plastic straws, the things we buy have an enormous impact on the environment. The Earth's natural resources, water supplies, and fragile ecosystems are suffering as a result of our lifestyle.

Factories make products to be shipped all over the world.

Factory production

Factories use a lot of energy and resources to make large quantities of objects to sell. Products are then shipped across the world for people to buy, producing even more greenhouse gases.

Fast fashion

Fashions come and go, but the environmental impact lasts for ever. Making cotton and polyester for clothes releases large amounts of greenhouse gases, while unwanted clothes end up in landfills.

Cotton field

Fabric dyes are sometimes dumped in rivers.

Trash that is thrown away mostly ends up in landfills.

! **WOW!**

In France, stores are **banned from destroying unsold food and clothes.** Instead, they give them to charity.

Waste disposal

Although we are becoming more conscious about recycling, waste that can't be reused or recycled is buried in the ground. This is a huge problem, since some waste takes hundreds of years to break down, and releases methane into our atmosphere.

Sustainable alternatives

Simple changes can help our environment. For example, switch from aluminium foil to reusable beeswax wraps, and from single-use plastic bottles to refillable steel or glass bottles.

Some zero wasters, such as environmental activist Bea Johnson, manage to keep all their year's waste in a single jar!

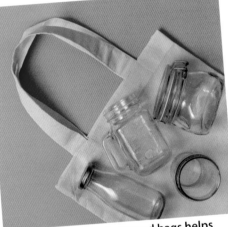

Reusing containers and bags helps the environment by reducing single-use waste.

Zero-waste living

By reducing what we consume and reusing as much as we can, it is possible to live a zero-waste lifestyle in which nothing is sent to a landfill.

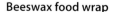

Beeswax food wrap

Deforestation

Forests around the world are threatened. Humans are chopping down trees at an alarming rate, and this is having a devastating effect all over the world.

Carbon storehouses

After oceans, forests store the most carbon on the Earth. Trees absorb carbon dioxide, preventing it from entering our atmosphere and contributing to climate change.

Forests cover 30 percent of land on the Earth.

Satellite image of the Amazon.

Amazon rain forest

The Amazon is the world's largest rain forest. Unfortunately, more than 20 percent of the Amazon has already been destroyed by humans, and the rate is increasing.

Clearing the land

Large areas of forest are cleared to create grazing land for cattle. Land is also used for plantations, such as soy and palm oil, which destroy animal habitats.

Logging

Trees are cut down to provide lumber and pulp, which are used for making paper, furniture, construction material, fuel, and other products.

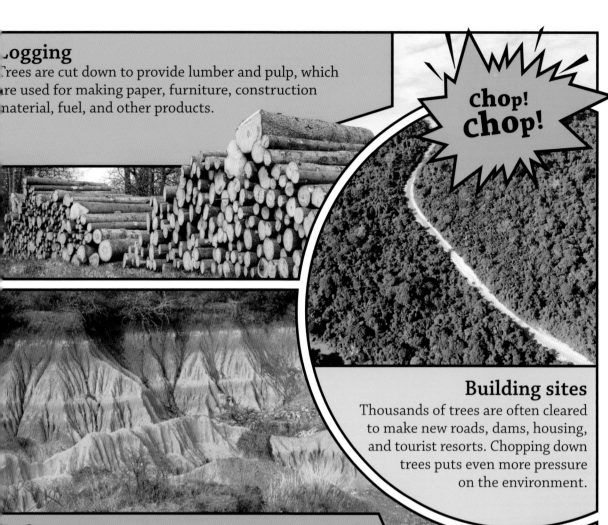

chop! chop!

Building sites

Thousands of trees are often cleared to make new roads, dams, housing, and tourist resorts. Chopping down trees puts even more pressure on the environment.

Soil erosion

The roots of trees hold soil in place, helping protect it from being eroded by rainwater. If trees are cut down, soil is easily washed away. This can block rivers, cause flooding, and contaminate water.

Reforestation

Planting more trees is an important step in our fight against climate change. Reviving cleared areas of forest can prevent more soil erosion, recover habitats, and reduce the amount of carbon dioxide in the atmosphere.

Planting new trees to combat climate change

Foodprint

Whatever you eat, your food has an impact on the environment. This can be measured using a foodprint. Although many of the processes involved in food production are invisible to the customer, they can take a huge toll on our soil, water, and air.

Food crops

Although it is considered an important staple food for many, rice is a key contributor to greenhouse gas emissions. Flooded rice fields produce large amounts of methane, a powerful greenhouse gas.

Rice fields also emit nitrous oxide, commonly known as laughing gas.

Cows release methane when they burp. On average, a single cow can burp up to 53 gallons (200 liters) of methane per year.

Livestock farming

Raising animals for food—such as meat, eggs, and milk—is one of the highest causes of deforestation and water pollution. Trees are cut down to make space for cows to graze. Livestock farming is to blame for 14.5 percent of global greenhouse gas emissions.

WOW!

It takes more than **264 gallons (1,000 liters)** of water to produce a **chicken breast.** That would fill a bath more than **12 times!**

Meat-free diet

Reducing the amount of meat you eat is a good place to start in the fight against climate change. Most plant-based foods have a much less damaging affect on the environment than those that come from animals.

These tasty falafels are made from chickpeas and herbs.

Set yourself a challenge to waste less food each week.

Food waste

Whether on farms and fishing boats, or in supermarkets and restaurants, food is wasted at each stage of production. When we waste food, we waste the energy and water used to produce it.

Alternative sources of protein

Two billion people around the world eat insects, and this alternative source of protein is becoming even more popular. Insects take up significantly less land, water, and feed than farm animals.

Crickets are 64 percent protein.

Polar crisis

As global temperatures rise, the Earth's poles are warming faster than any other place on the Earth. Disappearing snow, sea ice, and glaciers in the polar regions is having an effect around the world, putting the lives of many animals and people at risk.

Sea ice is melting at an alarming rate.

The Arctic

The Arctic is vulnerable to rising temperatures. Animals are losing their homes and the people who live there are feeling the effects of the changes.

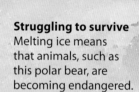
Struggling to survive
Melting ice means that animals, such as this polar bear, are becoming endangered.

Animals' habitats are melting.

The Antarctic

Rising temperatures are causing glaciers to melt. A decrease in Antarctic krill, small sea creatures, is threatening the lives of whales, seals, and penguins, who eat them to survive.

Global consequences

As land ice melts, sea levels rise which threatens low-lying land and coastlines. Changes in the poles could also cause changes to climate and weather patterns around the world.

Methane bubbles trapped in water

When melting takes place, methane is released into the atmosphere adding to the greenhouse effect.

Walruses in the Arctic

Habitat

Many animals rely on sea ice to survive. As their habitats change and disappear, walruses, polar bears, seals, and penguins are threatened.

REALLY?

The area of snow-covered **Arctic land** is expected to decrease by **10–20 percent** in the next 70 years.

Changing sea levels

Rising global temperatures are causing sea levels to rise. As the Earth gets warmer, ice sheets and glaciers melt, which adds more water to the oceans. The dramatic change in sea levels is one of the most worrying effects of climate change.

Thermal expansion

When water gets warmer, it expands. As climate change drives the Earth's temperature up, the oceans are getting warmer, which means they are getting bigger. This is causing sea levels to rise more.

Meltwater

In addition to in the oceans, there is a lot of ice on land in the form of ice sheets and glaciers. With the rise in global temperatures, land ice is beginning to melt. This is known as meltwater. As land ice melts, towns could become flooded.

Rising temperatures cause ice to melt and water to expand.

Ice on land is melting into the sea.

! WOW!

At the current rate, **sea levels will rise by 26 in (65 cm)** by the year 2100.

Absorbing carbon dioxide

As more carbon dioxide enters the atmosphere, our oceans soak it up. If the oceans reach the point at which they can no longer absorb any more gas, the amount of carbon dioxide in our atmosphere will increase even more.

he ocean is absorbing CO_2.

Habitat loss

Changing sea levels are having a devastating effect on wildlife, causing habitat loss, difficulty in surviving, and drastic changes to food supply.

Animals are losing their homes.

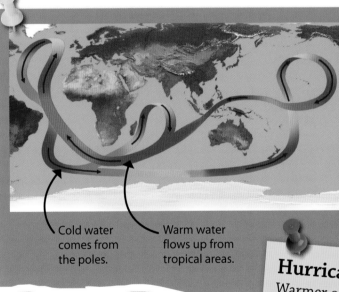

Cold water comes from the poles.

Warm water flows up from tropical areas.

Ocean current slowdown

When sea ice melts, it causes an increase in cold freshwater flowing into our oceans. This interrupts the circulation of saltwater, slowing down the ocean current. Our weather and sea life could be affected by the slowdown.

Hurricanes and tropical cyclones

Warmer ocean temperatures and higher sea levels are predicted to strengthen hurricanes and tropical cyclones, meaning they will cause even more damage when they hit land.

Climate change causes extreme weather.

Sinking islands

As the global temperature continues to warm up, ice is melting, oceans are expanding, and sea levels are rising. Hundreds of millions of people worldwide are at risk since they live on islands and in low-lying coastal regions.

Tuvalu Islands

Rising seas and coastal erosion are drowning low-lying areas of land. Two of Tuvalu's nine islands are on the verge of being swallowed by the sea. Tuvalu is the fourth smallest nation in the world and is home to 11,000 people.

FACT FILE

» **Number of islands:** Three reef islands and six true atolls

» **Location:** Oceania, Pacific Ocean

FACT FILE

» **Number of islands:** Chain of 26 atolls

» **Location:** South Asia, Indian Ocean

The Maldives

At the current rate of sea-level rise, the Maldives could be underwater by 210 The small coral islands are being flooded by extreme weather events.

Green sea turtles have fewer places to lay their eggs.

The Seychelles

This group of islands is sinking. Ocean warming is also having a devastating impact on their coral reefs. The people and wildlife that live in the Seychelles are threatened with the loss of their homes.

A warbler that lives on Aride Island, Seychelles.

FACT FILE

» **Number of islands:**
115 islands

» **Location:** South Asia, Indian Ocean

FACT FILE

» **Number of islands:**
More than 900 islands

» **Location:** Oceania, Pacific Ocean

The Solomon Islands

Five tiny islands have disappeared due to rising sea levels and erosion, and six more have had a large reduction in their coastlines. The population in the Solomon Islands is more than half a million people.

Future coastlines

Climate change is affecting the world's coastlines in a variety of ways. Rising sea levels, more frequent storms, and warmer ocean temperatures are having a devastating effect on the coast. The future of our coastlines is uncertain, with the lives of people and wildlife at risk.

Coastal erosion

Coastal erosion is speeding up. Land is being engulfed by the sea, which can damage buildings and infrastructure, costing a great deal to repair. As sea levels rise, the effects of coastal erosion are difficult to predict.

Gold Coast, Australia
Sand has been deposited in vulnerable areas of the beach as a buffer against future storms and coastal erosion.

Changing coastlines

With over 600 million people living in coastal areas that are less than 33 ft (10 m) above sea level, many coastlines need to be protected against the effects of climate change.

Buildings in New York City
In response to rising sea levels and storm events, coastal protection projects will ensure buildings and drainage can deal with frequent flooding.

River erosion in Bangladesh
Researchers have suggested building floating homes when land is eroded. The homes could be built to deal with extreme weather events.

The Sand Engine, Netherlands
The Sand Engine deposits sand along the coast to protect the low-lying land from sea water.

Coral bleaching

Colorful reefs made up of the skeletons of coral are at risk around the world. As the Earth's oceans heat up due to climate change, the algae that provide food for the coral are forced from the reef. The coral turns white and becomes much weaker.

The Great Barrier Reef

Bleaching in the world's largest coral reef has resulted in fish, turtles, and seabirds losing their habitats.

Algae
These give the coral its color and produce food for it. If the water gets too warm, the coral gets rid of the algae. This is called bleaching.

Healthy reef
Coral are animals, not plants! They form reefs that are some of the largest living things on the Earth.

Impact on humans

Millions of people rely on coral reefs. They protect coastlines from being worn down by waves, or getting flooded. The sea life that relies on coral for food or shelter is eaten by a lot of people. Coral, and the plants and animals that inhabit it, are also used to make some medicines. If reefs become damaged or die, it could affect people's homes, ability to get food, and health.

The bleaching of coral reefs could mean fewer fish to catch.

Sea life
Coral reefs are home to 25 percent of all marine species on the Earth. If the reef dies, many of these will lose their home.

Bleached reef
Coral without algae turns pale. It is weaker without its main source of food and is more likely to become diseased or die.

Extreme weather events

Changes to the Earth's climate are triggering variations in weather patterns. Extreme weather events—such as heat waves, droughts, storms, and flooding—are becoming more common and intense, having unpredictable and damaging effects.

Heat waves
Heat waves are periods of unusually hot weather lasting days or weeks. They are particularly dangerous to people who are very young, very old, or who have health problems.

Blizzards and hailstorms
Climate change has made the Earth's atmosphere warmer. A warmer atmosphere holds more water. When colder weather com so do blizzards and hailstorms because the atmosphere has more water stored up ready to be released. Hailstones can cause widespread dang and damage.

Floods

A warmer atmosphere stores more moisture, so rainfall is becoming more severe. This increases the likelihood of flood events, including flash floods that are unexpected and intense, as well as coastal flooding.

Droughts

A drought is triggered by a stretch of unusually dry weather and not enough rain. It can lead to a number of long-term problems for animals and people, including a shortage of water and damage to food sources.

Tropical storms

Warmer surface temperatures of the ocean and water in the atmosphere are causing tropical storms to become more intense. Climate change is also leading to more areas north of the equator experiencing them.

Grow your own

Growing your own vegetables is a big step toward helping save the planet. Without the need to ship food around the world, we can reduce the amount of pollution produced and the plastic waste that is thrown away. Start by growing these simple tomatoes.

Sow
Fill a seed tray with seed compost. Sprinkle tomato seeds onto the compost and cover with ¼ in (6 mm) more compost. Keep the seeds in a warm place. When the seedlings start to grow, move to a sunny position.

Transplant
When the plants are ready, carefully move two or three from the seed tray into a large container with drainage holes, filled with compost. Press the compost down around the plants. Make sure all the roots are covered.

Composting

Making your own compost is a great way to use up old vegetable peelings, grass cuttings, leaves, and cardboard. Keep filling your compost bin with kitchen and garden waste. After it has rotted, give your plants some compost to help them grow.

Do not put cat or dog poop, diapers, magazines, cooked food, oil, meat, or fish in your bin.

Attach your plant to a stake for support.

3

arvest
t the plants back in their sunny spot and keep em well watered as they grow. When tiny fruit gins to appear, feed the plants with tomato food help them ripen. Pick when they are bright red.

Other vegetables you can grow

Try growing these tasty veggies, too. If you don't have access to a yard, you can grow a lot of salad vegetables in pots on a windowsill or a balcony.

Growing carrots

Carrots
In spring or fall, plant your carrots in rows 1–2 ft (30–60 cm) apart. Seeds should be planted about $1/2$ in (1.25 cm) deep and 1–2 in (2.5–5 cm) apart.

Pick the carrots about 12 weeks after planting.

They are best when eaten soon.

Growing radishes

Radishes
Plant the seeds about 1 in (3 cm) apart, and around $1/2$ in (1 cm) deep. Keep the soil well watered—they grow quickly. Your radishes will be ready to pick in three to four weeks.

Animal life

Many animals around the world are being affected by climate change. Higher temperatures, rising sea levels, and changes in weather conditions will present new challenges for survival, including habitat loss and changes to the availability of food. Will our wildlife be able to adapt?

Hawaiian honeycreepers

Found in the higher altitudes of Hawaii, honeycreepers are usually protected by the cool temperature. As temperatures rise, malaria-carrying mosquitoes are biting and killing off these colorful birds.

Asian elephants

Asian elephants are sensitive to high temperatures. Climate change is making it more difficult for these elephants to find the large amounts of fresh water they need to survive because water sources are drying up.

Taking part

The Great Backyard Bird Count is a fun event that allows you to help create a real-time snapshot of bird populations. Counting and recording the birds you see in your backyard or local area allows scientists to know which birds are doing well and which are in trouble. Taking part is important as we face a changing climate.

All you need is a notebook, pen, and binoculars. Ask an adult to help you and always stay safe.

Sea turtles

Rising sea levels and warming temperatures are having a devastating impact on this endangered species. Disappearing nesting beaches, warming sand, and bleached coral reefs are affecting their chances of survival.

Adélie penguins

Adélie penguins feed on small sea creatures, called krill, which shelter under Antarctic ice. As the ice melts, the krill can't survive. The penguins must travel farther to find food, causing their chicks to wait longer for a meal.

Climate migrants

The effects of climate change are forcing people from their homes, cities, and even countries. Rising sea levels, extreme weather events, droughts, and water shortages are destroying communities. It is likely that more and more people will be forced to migrate (move to a new place).

In 2017, more than 8,000 firefighters fought against the flames in California.

California
Throughout California, rising sea levels, higher temperatures, and extreme wildfires are forcing people to leave their homes and move elsewhere.

Peru
Rising temperatures are causing glaciers in Peru to melt. As nearby lakes become swollen with meltwater, the risks of flooding are putting people nearby in severe danger.

The diminishing Pastoruri glacier at the Cordillera Blanca mountain range in Peru.

Millions of people are affected by flooding in Bangladesh.

Bangladesh

Coastal areas of Bangladesh are particularly vulnerable to flooding and typhoons (tropical storms), which are becoming more frequent as sea levels rise. Many Bangladeshis have already migrated to the capital, Dhaka, to escape the worsening effects of global warming.

Gavutu Island, Solomon Islands

Pacific Islands

Low-lying islands are being affected by rising sea levels, coastal erosion, and increased flooding. More than 40 percent of households predict that they will have to move to another country soon.

UNHCR

The United Nations High Commissioner for Refugees is taking action to support those affected by the impacts of rising global temperatures.

UNHCR refugee camp

West Africa

The rise in population, increase in water being used to grow food, and climate change have all contributed to Lake Chad shrinking in size by 90 percent. As conditions continue to worsen, people are forced to migrate.

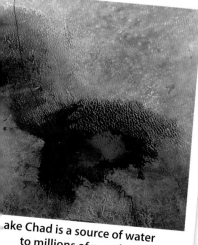
ake Chad is a source of water to millions of people.

Carbon footprint

Almost everything we do releases carbon into our atmosphere, from driving a car to buying food. Your carbon footprint is a measure of the total amount of carbon dioxide that you release in your day-to-day activities. Why not try walking to school to reduce your carbon footprint?

Switch it off

Turning off lights and unplugging devices can significantly reduce the electricity you use, which means less carbon dioxide is produced.

Buy local

Buying food that is grown locally can reduce your carbon footprint. Transporting food over long distances releases a lot of carbon dioxide into our atmosphere.

! REALLY?

Globally, we emit more than 2,500,000 lb (about 1,130,000 kg) **of carbon dioxide** every second.

Sustainable transportation

Walking, bicycling, or taking public transportation are environmentally friendly ways to travel, since they release less pollution.

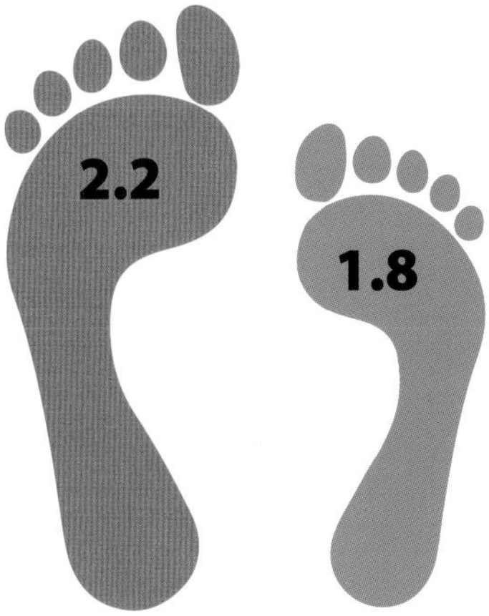

Ecological footprint

2.2

1.8

Your ecological footprint is the amount of the Earth's natural resources needed to support your lifestyle. This includes the amount of land and water needed to produce the things you use, such as food, paper, and energy.

Consider what you eat

Eating less meat and dairy is a simple way to reduce your carbon emissions. Vegetarian and vegan diets have considerably lower carbon footprints.

Earth defenders

People are important in the fight against climate change. Some individuals have supported projects to help lessen our impact on the environment, while others have encouraged people to stop damaging the Earth. We can all do things in our daily lives to help reduce climate change.

George Monbiot, United Kingdom
Since stopping a tree from being cut down at the age of eight, George Monbiot has written many books and articles about the environment. He has called for immediate action against climate change.

Leonardo DiCaprio, US
Actor Leonardo DiCaprio has used his fame to speak out against climate change. He often goes to protests and has set up an organization to support projects that provide solutions to climate change.

SKOLS
FÖR
KLIMA

The Green New Deal

In 2008, activists made a list of changes that countries could make to help the environment. They called this the Green New Deal. The list included clean or energy-efficient transportation, manufacturing, and buildings.

Some US politicians have argued in favor of the Green New Deal.

Greta Thunberg, Sweden
At 15, Greta Thunberg began skipping school to protest against climate change outside the Swedish parliament in 2018. Her speeches have inspired millions to become involved in the #climatestrike movement. In August 2019 she traveled in a solar-powered yacht to the US to give a talk since she wanted her trip to produce zero carbon.

Vandana Shiva, India
Named an environmental hero by *Time* magazine in 2003, Vandana Shiva started a national movement in India that championed environmentally friendly farming.

Ma Jun, China
After noticing the high levels of pollution in his country's capital city, Beijing, Ma Jun set up a plan to monitor the air there. He has written books and raised awareness about the effects of pollution.

School strikes

Millions of schoolchildren around the world are marching for their future. Fed up with waiting for politicians to act, children are demanding immediate action to address the climate crisis. As school strikes continue to grow, will the world start to listen?

! WOW!

The Global Climate Strike of 2019 took place in **185 COUNTRIES.**

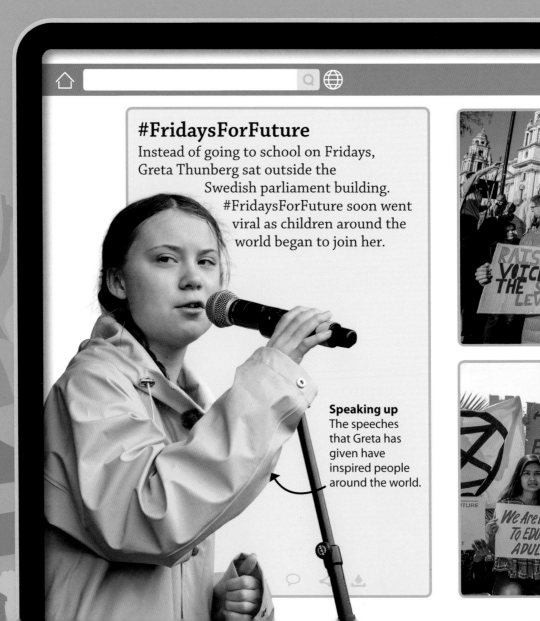

#FridaysForFuture
Instead of going to school on Fridays, Greta Thunberg sat outside the Swedish parliament building. #FridaysForFuture soon went viral as children around the world began to join her.

Speaking up
The speeches that Greta has given have inspired people around the world.

RAISE VOICE, THE SE LEVEL

We Are BUNK To EDUCAT ADULTS

Get involved

If you feel strongly about protecting your future against climate change, you can join the movement. Always ask an adult for permission and to help you stay safe. Follow the hashtags #FridaysForFuture and #ClimateStrike for more information about how you can get involved. FridaysForFuture is a peaceful striking organization.

Make a sign that stands out.

Having their say
Young people are asking the government to involve them in decision making linked to global warming, so that they can have a say in their future.

#YouthStrike4Climate

The #YouthStrike4Climate movement demands immediate action against the climate crisis. Schoolchildren around the world are participating in weekly or monthly protests for climate justice.

#GlobalClimateStrike

On September 20th, 2019 there was a Global Climate Strike, where more than 7.6 million people around the world followed the lead of schoolchildren and took to the streets to demand immediate action against climate change. Children missed school in order to strike.

Collective change

Climate change is the greatest environmental challenge the Earth has ever faced. As our planet continues to warm, both people and wildlife are affected. Many organizations are trying to protect our future against climate change. You can search online to find out more about these organizations.

World Wildlife Fund

If we fail to act against climate change now, one in six species are at risk of extinction. WWF is working with people in power to stop nature from being destroyed.

Friends of the Earth

Friends of the Earth believes that big changes can start small. Their Climate Action groups are suggesting local solutions to a global crisis, campaigning for a fairer, greener world.

Extinction Rebellion

As the Earth faces a global emergency that could lead to mass extinction, this organization is bringing people around the world together to express their concerns through nonviolent protesting.

Amazon Watch

Campaigning to protect the Amazon rain forest, this organization works with environmental groups to stop the destruction of the rain forest and support indigenous people.

Sierra Club

The Sierra Club brings people together to build a powerful and effective environmental movement. They believe that there is no time to waste in the fight against climate change.

Ocean Conservancy

As climate change threatens our oceans, Ocean Conservancy is developing solutions for healthy oceans and the many communities and wildlife that depend on them.

Greenpeace

In over 40 countries around the world, Greenpeace takes peaceful action to protect our Earth. Dedicated people come together to support a greener, healthier planet.

Renewable energy

Unlike fossil fuels, renewable energy is made from natural resources that won't run out, such as the sun, wind, and water. The energy produced generates few waste products and has a low impact on the environment. Many countries are reducing their use of fossil fuels by adopting renewable energy sources.

Hydro energy

Hydro energy is made when flowing water turns turbines, which generate electricity. Hydropower provides about 16 percent of the world's electricity.

Solar energy

Solar panels collect the sun's energy and turn it into electricity. The panels can be placed almost everywhere in the world, or even in space.

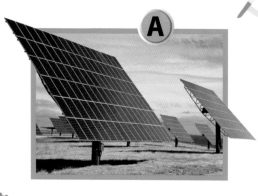

A

Wind energy

Wind turbines use the power of wind to spin the turbines and generate electricity. Wind farms are often built in places with strong winds, such as on hills, fields, or in the ocean.

B

C

1 What kind of energy do wind turbines produce?

2 What kind of energy is obtained from tides?

3 What kind of energy can be generated from the power of water in motion?

4 What kind of energy is derived from sunlight?

Wave power

A range of technologies has been developed to capture the energy from the movement of waves. Much like hydro and tidal energy, waves move up or down to spin a turbine, which generates electricity.

Waves generate a lot of energy.

Biomass energy

Biomass is organic material that comes from plant and animal waste, which contains energy absorbed from the sun. When burned, this energy is released and can be used as fuel.

F

Tidal energy

Similar to hydro energy, tidal energy uses the ocean's waves to spin turbines and produce electricity. This is more reliable than the sun or wind, since the tides are more predictable.

E

Geothermal energy

Below the Earth's surface are reserves of steam and hot water known as geothermal energy. Power plants use this energy to heat and cool buildings, or to generate electricity.

! WOW!

Iceland is the only country which **generates** all of its energy from **renewable sources.**

5

What kind of energy is harnessed from hot water below the Earth's surface?

6

What kind of energy can be derived from plant materials and animal waste?

Meet the expert

We ask some questions of Alice Fraser-McDonald, who is doing research into the levels of methane gas released by trees growing on landfill sites. She is studying for a PhD in Environment and Waste Management at the Open University.

Q: What are you studying at college?

A: My research looks at trees growing on landfill sites that are not accepting garbage anymore. I am trying to find out if the trees are giving out or taking in greenhouse gases, particularly methane.

Q: What inspired you as a child?

A: As a child I was really lucky to have lots of days out in the countryside and trips to the zoo with my family, and this meant that I became interested in nature and animals. I continued studying these subjects and I especially enjoyed biology and geography at school and college. I have continued developing these interests and that led me to become a PhD student.

Q: Why did you decide to focus your learning and research on trees?

A: I did a project on trees which I found really interesting and I particularly liked studying how trees can relate to climate change. There are so many trees on the planet, and they are involved in lots of different processes, so they are very important to study.

Q: What is your usual research day like?

A: I spend quite a few days in my office reading scientific research and sorting through the data I have collected. The most exciting days are when I get to go and visit field sites to take measurements from trees. On these days I take all my equipment to my sites and spend the day going from tree to tree measuring the methane and lots of other things like the temperature and how big the tree trunk is.

Q: How will the information be used to help with understanding climate change?

A: At the moment no one knows if the trees growing on these closed landfill sites are giving out or taking in greenhouse gases, so my research aims to find this out. When I have finished collecting data, I should know whether the trees are helping to slow down climate change by taking in methane, or contributing toward climate change by channeling methane from the garbage out to the atmosphere. Hopefully I can then say whether or not we should be planting trees on these sites.

Equipment used to measure greenhouse gases

Q: What are the best and worst parts of your research?

A: I really enjoy being able to go out to my field sites and take measurements. I like knowing that no one has done this research before so whatever I find out will be completely new. The worst part of my research is probably when it rains when I am out at my field sites!

Q: What special equipment do you use?

A: I use a greenhouse gas analyzer when I am collecting data in the field. It is a big yellow box that I connect with tubes to a chamber on the tree trunk. The gases in the chamber on the tree trunk go through the tubes and into the greenhouse gas analyzer. The analyzer tells me exactly which greenhouse gases they are and how much of each is in the chamber.

Q: Who else do you work with?

A: I work with other people at the college who help me with my research. I have supervisors who give me feedback and help guide my research. There are also technicians who help make my equipment and show me how to use it. I also have people who come into the field and help me take measurements from the trees; usually this is my family!

Q: What is your biggest wish for the future?

A: I am hoping that my research, along with lots of other climate change research, can help us understand climate change and greenhouse gases better and come up with ideas to try to slow down climate change in the future.

Alice measures the methane gas emissions from tree trunks and then writes up her findings.

Living with climate change

In the face of a changing climate, it is important that we learn to deal with the risks and consequences. By taking practical action, it is possible to minimize or prevent the damage that global warming will have on our lives. Play this game to learn more.

Roll a die and begin exploring.

START

Are you ready to learn about the effects of climate change? Find out what measures are being taken to adapt to the impacts of climate change and how technology can help us.

1 Hundreds of people living near the coast are being relocated because the rising sea level has led to high flooding risk. Miss a turn!

2 Coastal erosion

3 Some countries have started building floating structures as an adaptive measure. Roll the die again!

4 Floating apartments

5 Farmers are using drought-resistant crops. Move forward one space.

Corn

6 Factory pollution

7 The concentration of carbon dioxide (CO_2) in our atmosphere is the highest it has been in 3 million years. Move back three spaces.

8 Deforestation

The Paris Agreement

The Paris Agreement, opened to signatures in 2015, is the first global deal to fight the climate crisis. The Agreement requires all parties to adapt to the impacts of climate change.

UN conference in 2017 to discuss Paris Agreement goals

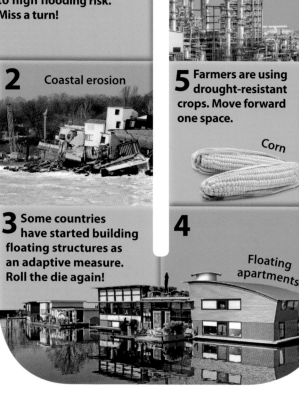

9 1,292 sq ft (120 sq m) of forest is cut down to make a tourist resort. Move back to the start.

10

11 Climeworks CO$_2$ capture plant

12 A CO$_2$ capture plant has been completed. Roll the die again! These plants capture atmospheric carbon with a filter, stopping it from entering the atmosphere.

16 Due to increased heat, there have been droughts and insect outbreaks. Miss a turn!

15

Mosquitoes

14 Seawall

13 In the US, Staten Island's 5 m (8 km) seawall project is finalized. Move forward two spaces.

17 MethaneSAT will be launched in 2022. Roll the die again! This satellite will make it possible to "see" methane emissions across the globe.

18 MethaneSAT

19 Drones help with reforestation. Move forward one space. BioCarbon, a UK-based company, has been using drones to spray tree seeds in damaged forests.

20 Drone

24 Many countries are burning less fossil fuels. Roll the die again! In 2017, Sweden produced more than half of its energy from renewable sources.

23 Forest fire

22

21 A forest fire breaks out due to prolonged heat waves. Move back one space.

25 Bullitt Center

26 A new block of smart buildings is built. Move forward one space. The Bullitt Center in Canada has solar panels across the roof that supply enough energy for the whole building.

Congratulations! You've finished the game.
There is, however, still a lot of work that needs to be done to effectively adapt to the changing climate.

FINISH

Add a scarf and wear gloves inside if it's really cold.

Avoid plastic

99 percent of plastic is made using oil and gas, which is responsible for 5 percent of global emissions. Ask your parents to switch from single-use plastics to reusable products.

Use wooden utensils.

Hot and cold

Heating your home uses a huge amount of energy. If you feel cold, don't turn up the heat—put on a cosy sweater to keep warm.

Open a window if you're too warm.

What can I do?

We are already feeling the effects of climate change around the world. There are plenty of simple changes we can make to help reduce our greenhouse gas emissions and combat climate change.

Air dry

Your clothes dryer uses electricity to generate heat, adding to your carbon footprint. Switching to a clothes rack or clothesline saves energy and can be more efficient on a sunny day.

Calculate your impact

Use an online carbon calculator to figure out exactly how much carbon you produce. Understanding where emissions come from will help you make small changes to reduce your affect on climate change.

Ask adults to help you.

Your voice matters

You can help in the fight against climate change. Use your voice to influence others to change their habits and make a difference.

Write a letter to your local government.

Ask an adult to help you learn how to sew a button onto a shirt.

Fix it

Today's throwaway culture is putting pressure on our planet, wasting resources and energy. Next time something appears to be broken, don't just replace it—try to fix it.

Facts and figures

Climate change is affecting the world around us. Here are some interesting facts you may not know about our warming world.

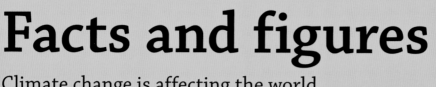

The planet's average **surface temperature** has **risen** by about $1\frac{1}{2}$°F (0.8°C) since 1880.

The **Amazon** rain forest is called the **"lungs of the world"** because it **removes** about **two billion tons** of carbon dioxide a year from the air. Cutting down forests is reducing this and also releases the CO_2 previously stored by the forest.

40%

or so of the carbon dioxide releases that are removed from the atmosphere are absorbed by the oceans.

36

cubic miles (152 cubic kilometers) of ice have been lost in Antarctica every year since 2002.

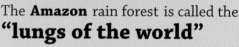

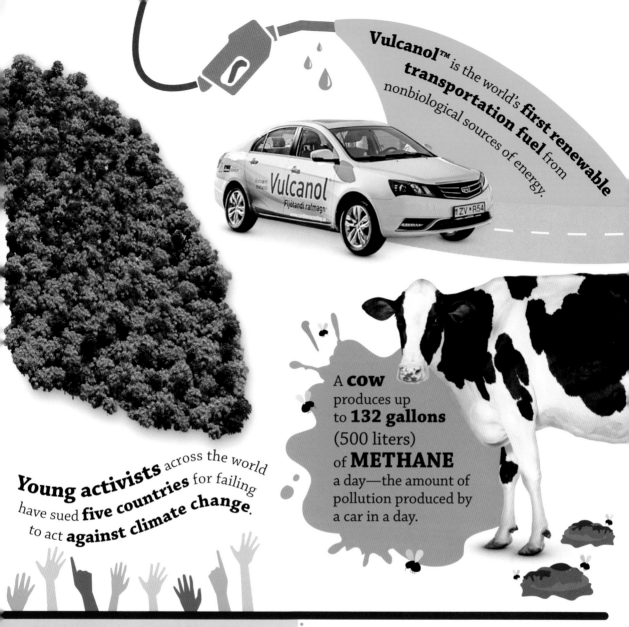

Vulcanol™ is the world's **first renewable transportation fuel** from nonbiological sources of energy.

A **COW** produces up to **132 gallons** (500 liters) of **METHANE** a day—the amount of pollution produced by a car in a day.

Young activists across the world have sued **five countries** for failing to act **against climate change**.

30 soccer fields per minute is the rate at which the world's tropical forests are shrinking.

195 countries have signed and adopted the Paris Agreement, committing to global climate action and adaptation to change, as well as the strengthening of climate goals.

Glossary

Here are the meanings of some words that are useful for you to know when learning about climate change.

activist A person who demonstrates to bring about change

asteroid A rocky object circling the sun

atmosphere Thick layer of gases that surround the Earth and protect the planet from the sun's rays

atoll Ring of coral reef surrounding a lagoon

biofuel A fuel produced from biomass

biomass Materials made from living organisms, such as animals and plants

carbon dioxide A colorless gas which is present in our atmosphere and is absorbed by plants. It is also released by burning fossil fuels. Its chemical symbol is CO_2

carbon footprint The amount of carbon dioxide a person's activities releases into the atmosphere

CFCs Gases that were used in refrigerators and aerosols. They caused damage to the Earth's ozone layer but have since been banned

climate The weather conditions in a certain area over a long period of time

deforestation The cutting down of trees to make land available, resulting in the destruction of forests

ecosystem A community of living things that interact with each other in their environment

enhanced greenhouse effect The heating up of the Earth as a result of increased greenhouse gas levels, due to human activity. Also known as climate change

energy What makes things happen. It is found in different forms, including heat, light, movement, sound, and electricity

erosion Breaking down of rock by water or weather

extinction When there are no more of a particular animal or plant species left alive anywhere in the world

fossil fuel Fuels formed by the decomposition of buried organisms. Oil, gas, and coal are fossil fuels. They contain large amounts of carbon and release carbon dioxide when burned for energy

fracking Forcing liquid at a very high pressure into the ground to extract oil or gas

global warming An increase in global temperature caused by the enhanced greenhouse effect

greenhouse effect The natural process in which gases in the Earth's atmosphere trap the sun's heat

greenhouse gas A gas in the Earth's atmosphere that absorbs the sun's heat. Carbon dioxide, methane, nitrous oxide, and water vapor are greenhouse gases

habitat The natural home of an animal or plant

Industrial Revolution The beginning of an era in which

achinery, powered by ssil fuels, was used to ake and transport things

frastructure Permanent ings, such as buildings, ads, and power supplies, at are needed for y-to-day activities

eltwater Water released the melting of snow and e, including from glaciers, a ice, or ice shelves

eteorite A piece of solid ck that has fallen to the rth from outer space

ethane A gas with no lor or smell, often used fuel. It is a powerful eenhouse gas that is oduced by cattle, burning ssil fuels, or when organic atter decomposes

icroclimate The climate a small area. It may be fferent from the climate the surrounding area

igration The movement people or animals from e place to another

itigation The action reducing the impact of mething

nrenewable energy ergy that comes from

sources that will run out or will not be replaced in our lifetime

oxygen A gas that is vital for life to exist on the Earth

ozone A form of oxygen which creates a layer around the Earth, called the ozone layer, and protects the Earth from the sun's rays. Ozone is pale blue in color

Pangea A supercontinent formed of all the Earth's land masses. It existed 335 million years ago, but broke apart to form the continents we know today

peaceful protest The act of expressing views and campaigning for change without using violence

pollutant A substance that pollutes the atmosphere or water

pollution The introduction of harmful materials into the environment

protest An action expressing an objection to something

reforestation Replanting an area with trees

renewable energy Energy produced from a source that

is naturally replenished and will not run out, such as wind, solar, tidal, or geothermal energy

sea level The average height of the sea when it meets land

single use Something that is used only once and then thrown away or destroyed.

stratosphere A layer of the Earth's atmosphere. The ozone layer can be found in the stratosphere

strike A refusal to work or go to school as a form of protest

sustainability Meeting the needs of people today, without damaging the ability of future generations to meet their needs

turbine A machine in which a wheel with blades is made to turn by the flow of liquid or gas. This turning motion produces energy

ultraviolet radiation A form of energy that travels in the sun's rays. Too much exposure can cause sunburn

zero waste Preventing any waste from being sent to landfills or from polluting the environment

Index

Acknowledgments

The publisher would like to thank the following people for their assistance in the preparation of this book: Caroline Stamps and Sophie Parkes for proofreading, Hélène Hilton for editorial assistance, Helen Peters for compiling the index, Jane Perlmutter for Americanization, and Alice Fraser-McDonald for the "Meet the expert" interview.

The publisher would like to thank the following for their kind permission to reproduce their photographs:

(Key: a-above; b-below/bottom; c-center; f-far; l-left; r-right; t-top)

1 iStockphoto.com: BrianAJackson. 2 Dreamstime.com: Alexandr Bazhanov (crb); Isabellebonaire (bl); Chernetskaya (br). iStockphoto.com: SDI Productions (bc). 3 Alamy Stock Photo: Daniel Reinhardt / DPA Picture Alliance (bc). Dreamstime.com: Erectus (bl). iStockphoto.com: Ekaterina_Simonova (cr). 4 Dreamstime.com: Viktoriia Kasyanyuk (bl). 4–5 Alamy Stock Photo: Anna Berkut (t). 5 Dreamstime.com: Alvaro German Vilela (clb); Wertes (crb). 6 iStockphoto.com: Ekaterina_Simonova (clb). 7 Alamy Stock Photo: Stocktrek Images, Inc. (t). Dreamstime.com: Corey A Ford (ca); Planetfelicity (cb). Science Photo Library: Claus Lunau (b). 9 Depositphotos Inc: Leonardi (cra). 10 Dreamstime.com: Nightman1965 (bl); Robwilson39 (br). Robert Harding Picture Library: FHR (cra). 11 Dreamstime.com: Chris Boswell (bl); Dutchscenery (crb). Robert Harding Picture Library: Alexandr Pospech (ca). 12–13 Alamy Stock Photo: Niday Picture Library. 13 Getty Images: Fox Photos (crb). Rex by Shutterstock: Cci (cra). 14–15 Getty Images: Per-Andre Hoffmann / LOOK-foto. 14 NASA: Goddard Space Flight Center (br); NASA Ozone Hole Watch (bc). 15 Depositphotos Inc: Zamula (cra). Dreamstime.com: Kevin M. Mccarthy (cr). NASA: Goddard Space Flight Center (bl, br); NASA Ozone Watch / Katy Mersmann (bc). 16 Dreamstime.com: Dezzor (cra); Kenneth Sponsler (cl). Pixabay: Quinntheislander (br). 17 123RF.com: Chokniti Khongchum (cr). Alamy Stock Photo: Alan Moore (clb). Getty Images: Bob Carey / Los Angeles Times (tl). 18 Alamy Stock Photo: Imaginechina Limited (crb). Dreamstime.com: Casadphoto (bl). Getty Images: Mint Images (cl). 18–19 Dreamstime.com: Maldives001 (tc). 19 Alamy Stock Photo: Jim Clark (clb). Dreamstime.com: Natasha Mamysheva (cr). Jacqui_J: (bc). 20 Dreamstime.com: Thamonwan Chulajata (crb); Vladvitek (tr); Smithore (cr). Getty Images: Tom Jakszat (tl). 21 Alamy Stock Photo: imageBROKER (cra); Willie Sator (c). Dreamstime.com: Alexander Naumov (bl). iStockphoto.com: Imantsu (cla). 22 Dreamstime.com: Ahavelaar (cb). 22–23 Dreamstime.com: Joyfull (ca).

23 Dreamstime.com: Rafael Ben Ari (cb); Sergii Koval (cra); Jaran Jenrai (br). 24 Getty Images: Rosemary Calvert (bl). PunchStock: Digital Vision / Tim Hibo (cl). 24–25 Robert Harding Picture Library: Michael Nolan (c). 25 Dreamstime.com: Erectus (cr); Damien Richard (tr). 26–27 Dreamstime.com: Odua (Background). 26 Dreamstime.com: Adfoto (cr); Alexander Nikiforov (bl). 27 123RF.com: Darko Komorski / kommaz (bc). Dreamstime.com: Birdiegal717 (tl); Eddygaleotti (cra). NASA: JPL (c). 28 Dreamstime.com: Ibrahim Asad (clb); Isabellebonaire (bl). Getty Images: The Asahi Shimbun Premium (cr). 29 Alamy Stock Photo: Galaxiid (clb). naturepl.com: Brent Stephenson (cra). Robert Harding Picture Library: Jean-Pierre De Mann (cr). 30–31 Getty Images: Chris Hyde. 31 Alamy Stock Photo: Frans Lemmens (crb). Dreamstime.com: Hsun337 (cra). Getty Images: Khandaker Azizur Rahman Sumon / NurPhoto (cr). 32 iStockphoto.com: Vlad61 (tr). 33 Alamy Stock Photo: WaterFrame. iStockphoto.com: SimonSkafar (tr). 34 Dreamstime.com: Frofoto (crb); Tom Wang (bl). 35 Dreamstime.com: Andrey Koturanov (cla); Jack Schiffer (bl). Getty Images: Ethan Miller (r). 36–37 Dreamstime.com: Airborne77 (tc). 36 Dreamstime.com: Dementevajulia (br); Nagy-Bagoly Ilona (cr). 37 Dreamstime.com: Pojoslaw (cra). iStockphoto.com: SDI Productions (crb). 38 Alamy Stock Photo: Photo Resource Hawaii (bl). Dreamstime.com: Cao Hai (br). 39 Dreamstime.com: Shane Myers (bl). Getty Images: Ralph Lee Hopkins (br). 40 Alamy Stock Photo: Matthias Kestel (bc). Dreamstime.com: Erin Donalson (cl). 40–41 Alamy Stock Photo: Rehman Asad (tc). 41 Alamy Stock Photo: imageBROKER (crb); NASA Image Collection (bl). Getty Images: The Asahi Shimbun (cra). 42 123RF.com: Prasit Rodphan (tr). Dreamstime.com: Pavel Losevsky (tc). 43 Dreamstime.com: Monkey Business Images (tc); Photographerlondon (br). 44 Alamy Stock Photo: DPA Picture Alliance (l); Steven Scott Taylor (c). 44–45 Alamy Stock Photo: Daniel Reinhardt / DPA Picture Alliance (c). NASA: Goddard Space Flight Center (Earth); MSFC / Bill Cooke. 45 Alamy Stock Photo: Alex Edelman / CNP / MediaPunch (tr). Getty Images: Gilles Sabrie / Bloomberg (l); Amanda Edwards / Wirelmage (c). 46 Getty Images: Michael Campanella (b). 46–47 Getty Images: Laurene Becquart / AFP (bc). Rex by Shutterstock: Facundo Arrizabalaga / EPA-EFE (c). 47 Alamy Stock Photo: Christoph Soeder / dpa picture alliance (tr). 48 Getty Images: Alfredo Estrella /

AFP (cra); Robert Ng / South China Morning Post (clb); Rodger Bosch / AFP (crb). 49 Alamy Stock Photo: Barry Lewis (cra); PJF Military Collection (clb). Getty Images: Pierre Andrieu / AFP (cla); Sajjad Hussain / AFP (crb). 50 123RF.com: Dimi Marinov / oorka (c). Dreamstime.com: Darren Baker / Darrenbaker (clb); Aleksandr Kiriak (cr). 51 Alamy Stock Photo: Michael Roper (c). Dreamstime.com: Aigarsr (tl); Irabel8 (tr); Smallredgirl (cra). 52 Lee Fraser-McDonald: (tl). Alice Fraser-McDonald: (bc). 53 Lee Fraser-McDonald: (r). 54 Alamy Stock Photo: Joern Sackermann (br). Dorling Kindersley: Stephen Oliver (ca). Dreamstime.com: Roman Budnyi (t); Andrew Zimmer (cb); Fabrizio Troiani (crb). Getty Images: Lukas Schulze (bl). iStockphoto.com: Georgeclerk (cr). 55 Alamy Stock Photo: travelstock44 (tc). Ball Aerospace: (c). Dorling Kindersley: Koen van Klijken (cla). Dreamstime.com: Alexsalcedo (cr); Yongsky (c); Elantsev (cb). Getty Images: Nic Lehoux / View Pictures / Universal Images (bl). 56 Dreamstime.com: Alexandr Bazhanov (cra); Inna Tarnavska (tl); Jo Ann Snover / Jsnover (tc); Chernetskaya (ca, br). iStockphoto.com: Alex Potemkin (cl). 57 Dreamstime.com: Darren Baker (tc); Korrawin Khanta (cr). iStockphoto.com: Tonivaver (br). 58 Dreamstime.com: Irabel8 (bl). 58–59 Dreamstime.com: Orlando Florin Rosu (l). 59 123RF.com: Eric Isselee / isselee (cr). Carbon Recycling International: (ca). 60 Dreamstime.com: Shane Myers (tl). 62 Alamy Stock Photo: Anna Berkut (tl). 64 Dreamstime.com: Alexandr Naumov (tl).

Cover images: Front: Alamy Stock Photo: FogStock l; iStockphoto.com: Amriphoto cra, Ra Hems bc, Photo5963 br, Picsfive c, Spawnscr; Bac Dorling Kindersley: Koen van Klijken cla; Dreamstime.com: Dezzor tr; iStockphoto.com: DNY59 cr; Robert Harding Picture Library: Jean-Pierre De Mann bl; Inside cover: 123RF.com: Eric Isselee / isselee crb; Dreamstime.com: Nida Picture Library cla, tr/ (2); Getty Images: Picsfive br/ (2); iStockphoto.com: Mphillips007 cb; Robe Harding Picture Library: Jean-Pierre De Mann cra

All other images © Dorling Kindersley
For further information see:
www.dkimages.com